¡A jugar! / Ways to Play

¡A HACER DEPORTES!
WE PLAY SPORTS!

By Leonard Atlantic
traducido por / translated by Eida de la Vega

Gareth Stevens
PUBLISHING

Please visit our website, www.garethstevens.com. For a free color catalog of all our high-quality books, call toll free 1-800-542-2595 or fax 1-877-542-2596.

Cataloging-in-Publication Data

Names: Atlantic, Leonard.
Title: We play sports! = ¡A hacer deportes! / Leonard Atlantic.
Description: New York : Gareth Stevens Publishing, 2018. | Series: Ways to play = ¡A jugar! |
In English and Spanish | Includes index.
Identifiers: ISBN 9781538205747 (library bound)
Subjects: LCSH: Sports–Juvenile literature.
Classification: LCC GV705.4 A43 2018 | DDC 796–dc23

Published in 2018 by
Gareth Stevens Publishing
111 East 14th Street, Suite 349
New York, NY 10003

Translator: Eida de la Vega
Editorial Director, Spanish: Nathalie Beullens-Maoui
Editor, English: Ryan Nagelhout
Designer: Bethany Perl

Photo credits: Cover, p. 1 Rawpixel.com/Shutterstock.com; p. 5 holbox/Shutterstock.com; pp. 7, 11 Brocreative/Shutterstock.com; p. 9 matimix/Shutterstock.com; pp. 13, 15 Studio 1One/Shutterstock.com; p. 17, 19 Rob Hainer/Shutterstock.com; p. 21 Marcel Jancovic/Shutterstock.com; p. 23 AS photo studio/Shutterstock.com.

Printed in the United States of America

CPSIA compliance information: Batch #CS17GS: For further information contact Gareth Stevens, New York, New York at 1-800-542-2595.

Contenido

Contents

A mis amigos
les encanta jugar.
¡Les encantan los deportes!

....

My friends love to play.
They love sports!

Mi amiga Jill tiene una pelota de fútbol.

....

My friend Jill has a soccer ball.

Nos encanta patearla.

We love to kick it.

Jugamos fútbol
en el parque.

We play soccer
at the park.

A Dave le encanta
jugar fútbol americano.

....

Dave loves
to play football.

Nos lanzamos
el balón.
¡Y tratamos de
atraparlo!

....

We throw it
to each other.
This is called
playing catch!

A mi hermano le gusta el béisbol.

....

My brother likes baseball.

17

Tiene su propio guante.

••••••••••••••••••••••••••••••

He has his own glove.

Me encanta jugar
a los bolos.

....

I love to bowl.

Tengo mi propia
bola de bolos.
¡Es rosada!

I have my own ball.
It is pink!

Palabras que debes aprender
Words to Know

(la) bola de bolos
bowling ball

(el) balón de fútbol americano
football

(el) guante
glove

Índice / Index